Frida Kahlo

A Proud Heritage The Hispanic Library

Frida Kahlo

An Artist Celebrates Life

Deborah Kent

The Child's World

The Child's World

Published in the United States of America by The Child's World®
PO Box 326 • Chanhassen, MN 55317-0326 • 800-599-READ • www.childsworld.com

Acknowledgments
   The Childs World®: Mary Berendes, Publishing Director
   Editorial Directions, Inc.: E. Russell Primm, Editorial Director; Pam Rosenberg, Project
   Editor; Melissa McDaniel, Line Editor; Katie Marsico, Assistant Editor; Matt Messbarger,
   Editorial Assistant; Susan Hindman, Copyeditor; Susan Ashley and Sarah E. De Capua,
   Proofreaders; Chris Simms and Olivia Nellums, Fact Checkers; Timothy Griffin/IndexServ,
   Indexer; Cian Loughlin O'Day and Dawn Friedman, Photo Researchers; Linda S. Koutris,
   Photo Selector
   Creative Spark: Mary Francis and Rob Court, Design and Page Production
   Cartography by XNR Productions, Inc.

Photos
   Cover: Detail from *Self Portrait with Monkey* by Frida Kahlo
   Cover photograph: Albright-Knox Art Gallery/Corbis
   Interior photographs: The Art Archive/Antochiw Collection/Mireille Vautier: 8; The Art
   Archive/Dagli Orti: 17 (National Palace, Mexico City), 27 (Museum of Modern Art, Mexico
   City); The Art Archive/Frida Kahlo Museum, Coyoacan, Mexico/Dagli Orti: 30, 32; Art
   Resource, NY/The Museum of Modern Art/SCALA: 9; Art Resource, NY/Schalkwijk: 15, 24;
   Bettmann/Corbis: 18, 21, 23, 28, 33; Bridgeman Art Library: 29 (Museum of Fine Arts,
   Houston, Texas), 34 (Index/Coleccion Banco Nacional de Mexico); Corbis: 13 (Farrell
   Grehan), 16 (Christie's Images), 31 (Reuters NewMedia Inc.), 35 (AFP); Getty Images: 7 (Omar
   Torres/AFP), 12 (Ed Clark/Time Life Pictures); Getty Images/Hulton|Archive: 11, 25, 26.

Library of Congress Cataloging-in-Publication Data
   Cataloging-in-Publication data for this title has been applied for and is available from the
   United States Library of Congress.

Chapter One

The Girl with Wings of Straw

At the corner of Londres and Allende Streets in the Coyoacán section of Mexico City stands a blue stucco house with many windows. Every year, thousands of people from all over the world visit the blue house. It was the birthplace of the beloved Mexican painter Frida Kahlo.

Written on one wall of the house is, "Here Frida Kahlo was born, July 6, 1910." In truth, she was born on July 6, 1907. She changed her birth date to match the beginning of the Mexican Revolution, which started in 1910. Throughout her life, Kahlo had a way of crafting reality to suit her own purposes. "I paint my own reality," she once wrote. "I paint whatever passes through my head without any other consideration."

Frida Kahlo's full name was Magdalena Carmen Frida Kahlo y Calderón. According to Mexican custom,

The birthplace of Frida Kahlo is now a museum that attracts thousands of visitors each year. Those who visit the museum are eager to learn more about Kahlo and her work.

she carried the surnames of both her parents. Her father, Wilhelm Kahlo, moved to Mexico in 1891 from Germany. Frida's mother, Matilde Calderón, was a Mexican of mixed Spanish and Indian heritage. Though their father was Jewish, the five Kahlo children were raised in their mother's Roman Catholic faith.

When Frida was six years old, she became sick. She had polio, a disease that affects the body's muscles. It took her nine months to recover. It was during this

President Porfirio Díaz ruled Mexico for nearly 35 years. Díaz was a dictator who allowed wealthy landowners to steal land from Mexico's poor **peasants.** A revolution broke out in 1910, and Díaz was overthrown. In 1911, a young teacher named Francisco Madero became Mexico's new president. However, Madero was not strong enough to hold the country together. He, too, was overthrown.

For the next 10 years, war swept over Mexico. Fighting raged in the north and in the south. Presidents came and went. One president held office for only 46 minutes! In the deserts of northern Mexico, the cowboy general Pancho Villa led the fighting. A Zapotec Indian named Emiliano Zapata led the rebel forces in the south. Zapata was greatly loved as a hero of the Mexican people. The Mexican Revolution was one of the bloodiest wars ever fought in the Western Hemisphere. More than one million people lost their lives during the revolution. The bloodshed did not end until 1920.

time that she created an imaginary friend who lived outside her window. Frida pretended that she slipped through a magic door in the windowpane to play with her friend in their magic world.

After Frida's bout with polio, her right leg was thin and weak. Other children called her Peg Leg because she walked with a slight limp. Frida's father encouraged her to believe in herself. As a young man, Wilhelm Kahlo had injured his head in a fall. For the rest of his life, he had **epilepsy.** Almost without warning, he would collapse and his body would shake uncontrollably. Despite his disability, he became a successful photographer. He assured his daughter that she could live the life she chose, despite her damaged leg. Years later, Frida wrote in her diary, "My childhood was marvelous, because although my father was

My Grandparents, My Parents, and I *portrays Kahlo's family tree. Her father was a Jew who moved to Mexico from Germany. Her mother was a mestizo, someone who has mixed Spanish and Indian heritage.*

a sick man, he was an immense example to me of tenderness, of work, and above all of understanding for all my problems."

The doctors told Frida's parents that exercise would help her regain her strength. In those days, Mexican girls were encouraged to cook, sew, and play quiet games. Instead, Frida boxed, wrestled, and played soccer with the boys. She loved to push her body to its limits. Many years later, she painted a picture of a little girl with wings made of straw. Streaming ribbons fasten the girl's dress to the ground. In her hand is a toy airplane. The painting shows how Frida felt as a child. She longed to fly like the airplane. But in reality, she was tied to the ground and her wings were only straw.

In 1922, when Frida was 15, she entered the **elite** National Preparatory School in Mexico City. Among Frida's classmates were the sons and daughters of doctors, lawyers, and political leaders. Frida joined a band of students who called themselves the Cachuchas. The Cachuchas were bright, creative, and rebellious. They delighted in playing pranks on their teachers. Once, they led a donkey through the school. Another time, they set off a firecracker outside the classroom of their most boring teacher. The boom rocked the building, but the teacher went on talking as though nothing had happened.

During Frida's first year at the school, a famous artist was hired to paint a **mural,** or wall painting, in the auditorium. The artist was Diego Rivera, one of the world's greatest muralists. He was an enormous man who wore a broad hat, a wide belt, and heavy cowboy boots. According to Rivera, one day Frida stepped quietly into the auditorium and asked

Kahlo grew up and attended school in Mexico City, the capital city of Mexico.

to watch him paint. For three hours, she sat there, silent and absorbed. Then she rose quietly and slipped away.

On September 17, 1925, Frida's life changed forever. She and a friend had spent the afternoon shopping and then boarded a city bus to go home. At a corner, the bus collided with a streetcar. In the first moments after the crash, Frida thought that nothing serious had happened. Later she wrote, "The first thing I thought of

Diego Rivera was one of the world's greatest muralists. He was hired to paint a mural at Kahlo's school.

Mexico has a long tradition of mural painting. Mexican murals often depict religious themes, battles, and other historic

scenes. Mexico's three greatest muralists were Diego Rivera, José Clemente Orozco, and David Siqueiros (above). All three wanted to see the Mexican people gain power and land, and their murals reflect these views.

was a pretty cup and ball toy I'd bought that day and had with me. I tried to look for it, convinced that all of this wouldn't have any major consequences." But in fact, her spine was broken in three places. Her right leg had 11 fractures, and her right foot was crushed. Most horrifying of all, a metal handrail had torn loose and pierced through her body. When she reached the hospital, doctors were sure Frida would die.

Brushes and Mirrors

"Death dances around my bed at night," Frida Kahlo told a friend as she lay in the hospital. Her body was encased in a plaster cast, and she was in constant pain. But she survived her terrible injuries. As the weeks dragged on, Kahlo longed to return to her former, active life. She thought that painting might fill the empty hours. Her mother rigged up an **easel** that allowed Frida to paint as she lay on her back. She also hung up a mirror. Kahlo studied her image in the mirror and began to paint.

After three months in the hospital, she was able to go home. Though she never went back to school, she remained friends with the Cachuchas, who were very involved in politics. Kahlo also made new friends, many of whom were artists. They believed that the poor people of Mexico and the rest of the world were being **oppressed** by the wealthy. To them, the **Communist** Party seemed to offer an answer. Kahlo and her friends read Communist writings and attended Communist rallies.

In the summer of 1926, Kahlo started painting portraits of herself. For the rest of her life, she expressed her feelings by creating self-portraits. These self-portraits were not realistic copies of what she saw in the mirror. Instead, they showed the way she felt about her body and her life. Painting helped Kahlo come to terms with the changes her body had undergone.

In The Bus, *Kahlo painted the people on that fateful bus ride that left her near death.*

In 1928, she visited Diego Rivera and showed him some of her pictures. Rivera was very impressed. He encouraged her to continue with her work. Kahlo told him she had many more paintings at home, and she invited him to look at them. They soon became romantically involved.

Kahlo's parents disapproved of Diego Rivera. He was 20 years older than their daughter, a Communist, and had been married twice before. Rivera was six feet tall (183 centimeters) and weighed more than 300 pounds (136 kilograms). Frida stood five feet three (160 cm) and weighed only 98 pounds (44 kg). Her father jeered that Rivera was an elephant courting a dove. But Frida's mother objected to Rivera even more. She was a devout Catholic and did

Memory *is one of many self-portraits painted by Frida Kahlo during her lifetime.*

Diego Rivera

Diego Rivera is considered the greatest artist Mexico has ever produced. He was born in the city of Guanajuato in 1886 and began drawing when he was only two. By the time he was three, he was painting. Before Diego could read, his father noticed his talent and made him his own studio. As a young man, Rivera studied painting in Spain, France, and Italy. He became famous in the 1920s for painting murals with political themes. In his paintings, he celebrated the traditions and spirit of Mexico's peasants. He showed how the Mexican people were oppressed by the wealthy and powerful.

During the 1920s and 1930s, Rivera was an active member of the Communist Party. Despite his political views, he created murals for rich families. One of Rivera's most famous murals outside of Mexico is *Detroit Industry*, found at the Detroit Institute of Arts. His mural depicting the history of Mexico (above) decorates the National Palace in Mexico City. Diego Rivera died in Mexico City in 1957.

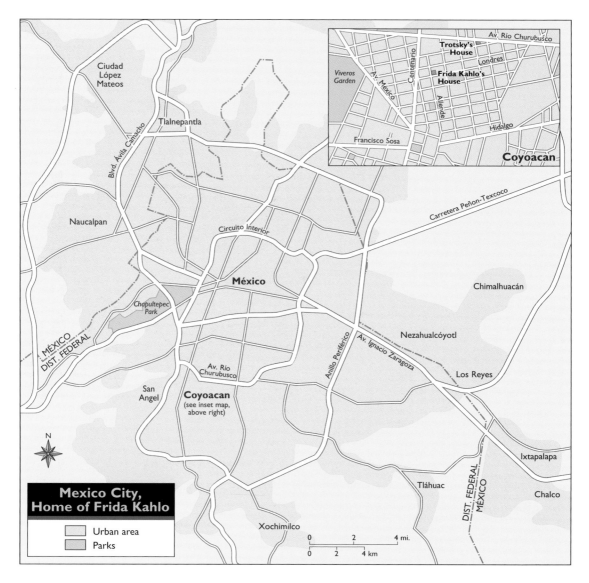

Frida Kahlo was born and raised in Mexico City.

not want her daughter marrying a Communist who did not believe in religion. Frida ignored her mother's warnings. She and Diego Rivera were married on August 21, 1929. Her father was the only member of her family to attend the wedding.

After their wedding, the couple moved to Cuernavaca, south of Mexico City. Friends flowed through their house, many staying for weeks or months at a time. Rivera painted by day and entertained everyone with stories late into the night. To their friends—and later to all of Mexico—the two artists were known simply as Frida and Diego.

After she married Diego Rivera, Kahlo began to take more interest in her Mexican heritage and began wearing the traditional clothing of Mexican Indian women.

From the beginning of their marriage, Rivera urged Kahlo to take an interest in Mexican traditions. She began to wear the traditional costumes of a Mexican Indian woman. She wore long, brightly colored skirts and put her hair in braids. She decorated her braids with combs and ribbons. Kahlo's traditional Mexican dress became her trademark.

In 1930, Kahlo and Rivera went to San Francisco, California, where Rivera was to paint a mural. At first,

Kahlo was shy amid the noise and glitter of an American city. Soon, however, she began to explore and to meet new people.

Kahlo and Rivera went to Detroit, Michigan, in 1932. There Rivera painted murals to celebrate the automobile industry. The following year, the couple moved to New York City. John D. Rockefeller, one of the richest men in the United States, had invited Rivera to paint a mural at Rockefeller Center. New Yorkers were fascinated by the big, smiling Mexican in the Stetson cowboy hat. They were also charmed by his tiny wife in her braids and Indian skirts. Kahlo lost her shyness. She delighted everyone with her warmth and wit.

New Yorkers flocked to watch Rivera at work, perched on his platform high above the street. Sometimes Kahlo sat below the platform, singing Mexican songs with her friends. "Carmen Frida Kahlo Rivera is a painter in her own right, though very few people know it," one reporter wrote. Newspaper stories often called her "Little Frida" as though she were an amusing child.

Rivera's Communist friends were outraged that he was painting a mural for Rockefeller. The Rockefellers stood for everything the Communists despised. The Rockefellers were immensely rich and powerful. They hired thousands of workers for pitifully low wages.

Diego Rivera (right) at work on the mural at Rockefeller Center.

But Rivera had not forgotten his Communist beliefs. In the mural, he included the figure of the Russian Communist leader Vladimir Lenin. Rockefeller ordered Rivera to remove Lenin's portrait. When Rivera refused, Rockefeller had the whole mural destroyed. Rivera and Kahlo were **devastated.**

Kahlo begged to go back to Mexico. At first, Rivera refused, and the couple had many fierce arguments. Finally, late in 1933, they returned to Mexico City.

Chapter Three

The House with the Bridge

Frida Kahlo and Diego Rivera had a stormy marriage. They were both strong willed, and they fought often and bitterly. Rivera had numerous love affairs, which hurt Kahlo deeply. Kahlo also had many love affairs. Despite these tensions, Kahlo and Rivera cared for one another very much. They enjoyed being together, and they admired and encouraged each other's work. In her diary, Kahlo once wrote a note to Rivera: "I'd like to paint you, but there aren't enough colors."

The couple moved into a blue stucco house that Rivera had built. A spiral stairway led from the inner patio to the studio where Kahlo painted. A bridge connected her studio to Rivera's. In this way, they managed to share their lives while still having plenty of privacy.

Frida Kahlo and Diego Rivera loved each other but had a very stormy marriage.

In this self-portrait, Kahlo is pictured with a monkey. The monkeys and dolls in many of her self-portraits are stand-ins for the children she was unable to have.

Kahlo's old injuries continued to plague her. Her medical bills were enormous and un-ending. Over her lifetime, she had 32 operations. Some-times her pain was almost unbearable. The accident also left her unable to have children. Kahlo grieved that she and Rivera could never have a child together. In many of her self-portraits, Kahlo appears with dolls or monkeys that represent the babies she never had.

Artists and political activists often visited their blue house. For several months in 1938, the Russian Communist Leon Trotsky lived in the house in Coyoacán where Kahlo was born. Trotsky had quarreled with

Communist leaders in Russia and fled to Mexico. When he was killed in 1940, the Mexican police accused Kahlo and Rivera of his murder. They were both arrested and questioned before the charges were dropped.

In 1938, a small gallery in New York put on an **exhibition** of Kahlo's work. At the show, movie actor

An Enemy of the Party

In 1917, a revolution established a Communist government in Russia. Leon Trotsky (right) was a powerful leader in the country's Communist Party. During the 1930s, Josef Stalin seized control of the party and forced Trotsky to flee the country. Trotsky made his new home in Mexico City. Stalin's secret police murdered him there in 1940.

Edward G. Robinson bought four of her paintings. This was Kahlo's first major sale. The following year, the French artist Andre Breton arranged an exhibition of Kahlo's work in Paris. Rivera urged her to attend. He wrote to her, "Take from life all that she gives you, whatever it may be, provided it is interesting and can give you some pleasure." So Kahlo went to Paris. The Louvre, the most famous art museum in that artistic city, purchased one of her paintings.

Famous actor Edward G. Robinson poses at his home in Beverly Hills, California. He bought four of Kahlo's paintings in 1938 at an exhibit of her work in New York City.

The difficult marriage between Kahlo and Rivera

ended in divorce in 1940. Though they lived apart, the two artists remained close and saw each other often. For Kahlo, the divorce was heartbreaking. It inspired one of her best-known paintings, *The Two Fridas*. In this picture, she painted a pair

After her divorce from Diego Rivera in 1940, Kahlo was inspired to create The Two Frida's, *one of her most famous works.*

of self-portraits, the Frida whom Rivera loved and the Frida he rejected. The two Fridas are linked by their clasping hands. In her misery, Kahlo is holding her own hand to comfort herself.

Kahlo and Rivera couldn't live apart for long. In December 1940, they married for the second time. They went on, fighting, working, and loving each other, until the end of Kahlo's life.

Chapter Four

Alegría

Kahlo holds a monkey, one of the many animals that filled her home.

As the years passed, Kahlo's physical pain increased. It grew harder and harder for her to leave her home. Sometimes she was so weak she had to stay in bed. Propped against her pillows, she painted in bed as she had right after the accident. For company, Kahlo filled the house with animals. Parrots squawked and cackled in the patio, and monkeys leaped

Emmy Lou Packard (right) was one of Frida Kahlo's many friends. Packard was an artist who worked for a time as Diego Rivera's assistant. She also lived with Rivera and Kahlo in Mexico early in her career.

and chattered. A pair of turkeys strutted about, hissing at visitors. A tame chipmunk sat on Kahlo's shoulder and ate seeds from her hand. She even had a pet eagle.

Though Kahlo could seldom go to parties now, parties came to her. Friends flocked to the blue house. They admired her latest paintings and brought treats for her monkeys. They sat in the patio, listening to Kahlo's stories and singing the Mexican songs she loved. Though she was ill, Kahlo's spirit was strong.

Frida Kahlo worked in this studio in her Blue House. Rivera lived with Kahlo in the Blue House after they remarried in 1940.

Those who knew and loved her spoke of Kahlo's *alegría*. Alegría is the Spanish word for "happiness."

In 1943, Kahlo began to teach at La Esmeralda, a new art school in Mexico City. The school was free, and many of the students came from the city's poorest neighborhoods. When Kahlo's health kept her from traveling to the school, she invited the students to her home. They set up their easels in her patio and painted while she rested in her room. Then she came out to comment on their work.

In 1944, Frida Kahlo began to keep a diary (held by a woman, right), a habit she continued for the rest of her life. Her diary was far more than a record of daily events. In it she looked back over her life, describing and pondering events of the past. She also wrote about political issues and her many love affairs. Some pages seem to be lists of words or phrases that appealed to her for unknown reasons. Kahlo's diary also served as a sketchbook. Its pages include many drawings in ink or crayon. In some places, she splashed drops of ink on a page to make strange, dreamlike images.

Friends read Kahlo's diary soon after she died. Apparently they did not want some of her writing to be revealed to the public. They tore out and destroyed several pages. The secrets of Frida Kahlo's diary will be kept forever.

Kahlo went to New York in 1946 for an operation on her spine. At first, the surgery seemed to help her, but soon her condition worsened. Powerful drugs controlled her intense pain. Eventually, Kahlo became addicted to painkillers.

In April 1953, one of her friends organized Kahlo's first and only Mexico City exhibition. Her paintings were displayed at the city's Gallery of Contemporary Art. As opening night approached, Kahlo's doctors warned her to stay home. She was too weak, they claimed, to leave her bed. Kahlo had other ideas, though, and she and her friends worked out a plan.

The evening that the exhibition opened, Kahlo's admirers packed the gallery. Amid the paintings, they saw a magnificent four-poster bed. The bed was decorated with photographs

During the last years of her life, Kahlo was often too weak to leave her bedroom. She continued to paint, even though she was often in too much pain to get out of her bed.

and molded figures. Carved skulls and skeletons dangled from the bedposts. The bed itself was a remarkable work of art.

Suddenly, the guests heard the wail of sirens. An ambulance escorted by motorcycles drove up in front of the gallery. Friends lifted Kahlo out of the ambulance. They carried her into the hall and laid her on the bed. She was dressed in her traditional costume and jewelry. One by one, people lined up to speak to her. "I am not sick," Kahlo told a reporter. "I am broken, but I am happy to be alive as long as I can paint."

A man works on an artificial leg. At first, Kahlo refused to wear her artificial leg after doctors amputated her leg to save her life.

Kahlo's exhibition was her farewell to her adoring public. After that splendid night, her health declined rapidly. A stubborn infection ate away at her right leg. Doctors felt they must **amputate** Kahlo's leg to save her life. She was terrified but tried to face the operation bravely. In her diary, she drew a picture of her legs

33

The Fruit of the Earth *is a still life painted by Kahlo.*

resting on a pedestal, her right foot missing. Under the drawing she wrote, "Feet! What do I want them for if I have wings to fly?"

After the operation, Kahlo was deeply discouraged. Rivera sat for hours at her bedside, but she hardly spoke to him. At first, she refused to wear her **artificial** leg. After a few months, however, her spirit rallied. She wore the artificial leg and learned to walk short distances. A pair of red velvet boots added new flair to her costume. With the boots, Kahlo called special attention to her feet, the real one and the one made of plastic.

By the spring of 1954, Kahlo began to paint again. Some of her pictures were still lifes, paintings of fruits and vegetables. Her last finished painting shows brightly colored slices of watermelon. At the bottom of the picture she wrote, *Viva la vida*—"long live life!" Early in July, Frida contracted pneumonia, a lung disease. Weak as she was, she could not fight off the illness. Her final diary entry shows a dark angel rising to the sky. "I hope the exit is joyful," she wrote, "and I hope never to come back." She died on July 13, 1954.

Frida Kahlo lives on in the hearts of millions. Her paintings hang in some of the world's finest museums. They appear on T-shirts, notepaper, and even a U.S. postage stamp. Kahlo's admirers continue to celebrate her daring and originality. Kahlo once wrote to Rivera, "I leave you my portrait so that you will have my presence all the days and nights that I am away from you." She left a lifetime of portraits, and her presence has never faded.

The U.S. Postal Service's commemorative stamp of Frida Kahlo is unveiled during a ceremony at the Mexican Cultural Institute in Washington, D.C., in July 2001.

1886: Diego Rivera is born in Guanajuato, Mexico.

1891: Wilhelm Kahlo, Frida's father, moves to Mexico from Germany.

1907: Frida Kahlo is born in Coyoacán, a section of Mexico City, on July 6.

1910: The Mexican Revolution breaks out.

1913: Frida Kahlo becomes sick with polio.

1920: The Mexican Revolution finally comes to an end.

1922: Kahlo enrolls at Mexico City's National Preparatory School. She watches Diego Rivera paint a mural at the school.

1925: Kahlo is severely injured in a bus accident.

1926: Kahlo starts painting portraits of herself.

1928: Kahlo visits Diego Rivera to show him some of her paintings.

1929: Frida Kahlo and Diego Rivera are married in Mexico City on August 21.

1930: Kahlo and Rivera travel to San Francisco, where he paints a mural.

1933: Kahlo and Rivera go to New York, where Rivera works on a mural for Rockefeller Center.

1938: A gallery in New York hosts an exhibition of Kahlo's paintings.

1939: An exhibition of Frida Kahlo's work is put up in Paris.

1940: Kahlo and Rivera are divorced, and Kahlo paints *The Two Fridas*. They remarry in December.

1943: La Esmeralda, a new art school in Mexico City, hires Kahlo as a teacher.

1944: Kahlo begins to keep a diary filled with memories and drawings.

1946: Kahlo has a major operation on her spine.

1953: The Gallery of Contemporary Art hosts Kahlo's only Mexico City exhibition.

1954: Kahlo dies at her home in Mexico City on July 13.

1955: Rivera gives Kahlo's house in Coyoacán to the public as the Frida Kahlo Museum.

2001: A commemorative stamp of Frida Kahlo is issued by the U.S. Postal Service in honor of her life and work.

amputate (AM-pyuh-tate) To amputate an arm or leg is to cut it off for medical reasons. Doctors amputated Frida Kahlo's right leg in an attempt to save her life.

artificial (ar-ti-FISH-uhl) Something is artificial if it is human-made. After Frida Kahlo's right leg was amputated, she was given an artificial leg to replace it.

Communist (KOM-yuh-nist) A Communist is someone who believes that the government should distribute wealth equally to all the people. Diego Rivera and Frida Kahlo were active Communists in the 1930s.

devastated (DEV-uh-stay-tid) To be devastated is to be terribly hurt and upset. Diego Rivera and Frida Kahlo were devastated when Rockefeller destroyed Rivera's mural in New York.

easel (EE-zuhl) An easel is a frame to support a painting while the artist works on it. Frida Kahlo's mother rigged up an easel so she could paint while she lay in bed.

elite (i-LEET) Something that is elite is among the best of its kind. When Frida Kahlo was 15, she began attending an elite preparatory school.

epilepsy (EP-uh-lep-see) Epilepsy is a disease that causes sudden violent shaking attacks or blackouts. Frida Kahlo's father had epilepsy.

exhibition (ek-suh-BISH-uhn) An exhibition is a show of an artist's work. Frida Kahlo's first exhibition was in New York City in 1938.

mural (MYOO-ruhl) A mural is a large painting on the wall of a building. Diego Rivera was famous for painting murals.

oppressed (uh-PRESSED) To be oppressed is to be crushed or held down. Frida Kahlo and her friends believed the poor were oppressed by the wealthy.

peasants (PEZ-uhnts) Peasants are poor farmers or farm laborers. President Díaz allowed wealthy landowners to steal land from Mexico's poor peasants.

Books

Cruz, Barbara. *Frida Kahlo: A Portrait of a Mexican Painter.* Springfield, N.J.: Enslow Publishers, 1996.

Laidlaw, Jill A. *Frida Kahlo.* Danbury, Conn.: Franklin Watts, 2003.

Morrison, John. *Frida Kahlo.* Philadelphia: Chelsea House, 2003.

Venezia, Mike. *Frida Kahlo.* Danbury, Conn.: Children's Press, 1999.

Woronoff, Kristen. *Frida Kahlo.* Woodbridge, Conn.: Blackbirch Press, 2002.

Web Sites

Visit our Web page for lots of links about Frida Kahlo:
http://www.childsworld.com/links.html

Note to parents, teachers, and librarians: We routinely check our Web links to make sure they're safe, active sites—so encourage your readers to check them out!

About the Author

Deborah Kent grew up in Little Falls, New Jersey, and received her bachelor's degree from Oberlin College. She earned a master's degree from Smith College School for Social Work and worked as a social worker before becoming a full-time writer. She is the author of 18 young-adult novels and more than 50 nonfiction titles for children. She lives in Chicago with her husband, children's author R. Conrad Stein, and their daughter, Janna.